Study and design of a s

Zackaria Yamar Ndiaye

Study and design of a simulator based on a process language

ScienciaScripts

Imprint

Any brand names and product names mentioned in this book are subject to trademark, brand or patent protection and are trademarks or registered trademarks of their respective holders. The use of brand names, product names, common names, trade names, product descriptions etc. even without a particular marking in this work is in no way to be construed to mean that such names may be regarded as unrestricted in respect of trademark and brand protection legislation and could thus be used by anyone.

Cover image: www.ingimage.com

This book is a translation from the original published under ISBN 978-613-8-43055-1.

Publisher:
Sciencia Scripts
is a trademark of
Dodo Books Indian Ocean Ltd. and OmniScriptum S.R.L publishing group

120 High Road, East Finchley, London, N2 9ED, United Kingdom
Str. Armeneasca 28/1, office 1, Chisinau MD-2012, Republic of Moldova, Europe

ISBN: 978-620-6-09364-0

Copyright © Zackaria Yamar Ndiaye
Copyright © 2023 Dodo Books Indian Ocean Ltd. and OmniScriptum S.R.L publishing group

Table of contents :

Chapter 1	2
Chapter 2	3
Chapter 3	4
Chapter 4	8
Chapter 5	12
Chapter 6	29
Chapter 7	46

1 Introduction

Simulation, in general, is one of the branches of computer science that has enjoyed a boom over the past 10 years. It provides satisfactory results for understanding, controlling and predicting real-world phenomena. Simulation involves creating a computer model from a real or theoretical system, and then running it to analyze the results.

Multi-agent simulation is based on the idea that it is possible to represent in computer form the behavior of autonomous entities and the phenomena resulting from their interactions. In this way, multi-agent systems offer the possibility of representing individuals, their behaviors and their interactions.

In this DEA dissertation, we propose to design a multi-agent simulation model (section 3) with a language of concurrent processes based on a concrete application (the Rapsodie project of the UR RAP). In section 4, we will give a brief presentation of this model, focusing in particular on its difficulties in relation to the tools used to implement it. In the following section, we will detail our proposals to overcome these constraints, then the implementation of these proposals will be detailed in section 6, then in section 7, we will make suggestions for a better implementation of the model in the future, finally section 8 will conclude this dissertation.

2 Issues

The aim of this DEA internship is to design a distributed simulation model using a concurrent process language, in particular Erlang, and to analyze its feasibility, with a view to achieving a higher level of complexity. Our approach will be to show that this model can be adapted to the types of applications required to monitor the evolution of a fish population in space and time in the face of multiple environmental disturbances.

This work will be based in part on the model initiated in the Rapsodie project, which has shown certain limitations linked to a slow simulation speed and rapid saturation due to the cumbersome nature of the chosen simulation tool (Cormas).

The aim is to deepen and enrich the conceptual work that has been initiated, and above all to show the relevance and interest of the choice of Erlang in the face of the difficulties encountered.

3 Multi-agent systems

Multi-agent systems are often presented as being at the crossroads of two major disciplines: distributed artificial intelligence and artificial life [Paul et al. 2002].

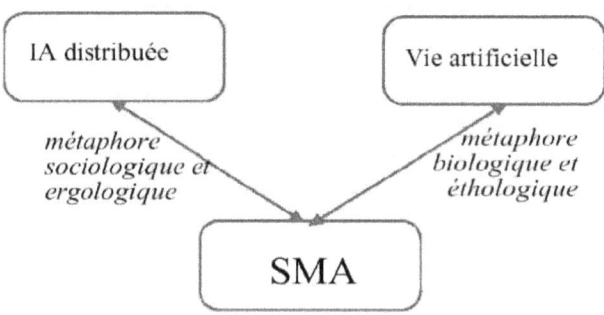

Figure 1: Multi-agent system approach

Distributed artificial intelligence is the study and design of organizations made up of several agents (see next), with the aim of solving complex problems [FERBER 1995]. It adds a new dimension to the field of artificial intelligence, which used to focus on imitating the behavior of an individual, or part of an individual, in a specific domain. One application of artificial intelligence is the Expert System: a computer program that reproduces the behavior of a human expert performing an intellectual task in a specific field. We speak of distributed artificial intelligence in the sense that the decision-making system is not centralized, as in the case of Expert Systems. In other words, it is also defined as "the study and design of organizations of artificial agents to obtain intelligent systems" [DROGOUL1993].

The aim of artificial life is to understand and model systems endowed with life. The individuals in the system are capable of surviving, adapting and reproducing in an often hostile environment. It is in fact an abstraction of the principles underlying the organization of living organisms and their implementation with computer tools so that they can be studied and tested.

We'll use Jacques FERBER's definitions [FERBER 1995] as a basis for clarifying the terms and concepts most commonly used in multi-agent simulation.

3-1 Definitions

An agent: This term is of very general application and has been defined in a variety of ways. According to FERBER, an agent is a physical or virtual entity:
1- who is able to act in an environment ;
2- that can communicate directly with other agents;
3- which is driven by a set of tendencies (in the form of individual objectives or a satisfaction or even survival function, which it seeks to optimize);
4- with its own resources;
5- is able to perceive (but in a limited way) its environment;
6- which has only a partial representation of this environment (and possibly none at all);
7- with skills and services;
8- which can eventually be reproduced;
9- whose behavior tends to satisfy its objectives, taking into account the resources and skills at its disposal, and according to its perceptions, representations and the communications it receives.

To illustrate the diversity of agent definitions, we will give two more:
According to DEMAZEAU, an agent is a real or virtual entity whose behavior is autonomous, evolving in an environment, capable of perceiving it, acting on it and interacting with other agents [DEMAZEAU 1996].

According to WOOLDRIDGE, an agent is a computer system capable of acting autonomously and flexibly in the environment [WOOLDRIDGE 1998]. By flexibility we mean reactivity, a certain degree of proactivity and a social capacity.
- Reactivity: agents must be able to perceive their environment and respond in a timely fashion.
- Proactivity: the agent must demonstrate proactive and opportunistic behavior, while being able to take the initiative at the right moment.
- Social skills: the agent must be able to interact with other agents when the situation calls for it, in order to complete his/her tasks or help others accomplish theirs.

The definition that best describes the agents we'll be using in our model is FERBER's definition of communicating agents. A communicating agent is defined by FERBER as a computer entity that :
1- is located in an open IT system (a set of heterogeneous applications, networks and systems);
2- can communicate with other agents;
3- is driven by its own set of objectives;
4- has its own resources;
5- has only a partial representation of the other agents;
6- has skills (services) that it can offer to other agents;

7- behaves in such a way as to meet its objectives, taking into account the resources and skills at its disposal and the representations and communications it receives.

We note the emergence of two approaches, namely the cognitive approach and the reactive approach, which characterize agents by the following question: should we conceive of agents as already intelligent entities, i.e. capable of solving certain problems by themselves, or should we assimilate them to very simple beings reacting directly to changes in the environment?

The cognitive approach: this approach favors a sociological vision of the organization. It was born of the desire to understand and grasp the social aspect of knowledge. These agents are generally highly complex. They represent knowledge about themselves, others and the world around them. They control their environment.

The reactive approach: This approach takes a completely different line from the cognitive approach. The reactive agent has no representation of his environment, of others or of himself. This means they cannot control their behavior or actions. He very often reacts under the effect of stimuli received from the environment. Taken individually, it has no intelligence. However, its interaction with others can give rise to intelligent behavior.

A multi-agent system: a multi-agent system (MAS) is a system made up of the following elements :
1- an environment E, a space that generally has a metric ;
2- a set of objects O. These objects are situated, i.e. it is possible, at a given moment, to associate a position in E with any object. These objects are passive, i.e. they can be

perceived, created, destroyed and modified by agents;

3- a set A of agents, which are particular objects (A included in O), representing the system's active entities;
4- a set of relationships R that link objects (and therefore agents) together;
5- a set of operations Op enabling agents in A to perceive, produce, consume, transform and manipulate objects in O ;
6- operators responsible for representing the application of these operations and the world's reaction to this attempted modification, known as the law of the universe.

Another definition of multi-agent systems: A multi-agent system is a distributed system composed of a set of agents. Unlike artificial intelligence systems, which to some extent simulate human reasoning capabilities, MAS are designed and implemented, ideally, as a set of agents interacting, more often than not, according to modes of cooperation, competition and coexistence.

SMAs are characterized by :
- each agent has limited information or problem-solving capabilities, so each agent has a partial point of view;
- there is no global control of the multi-agent system;
- data are decentralized ;
- and the calculation is asynchronous.

4 Analysis of existing

4-1 Presentation of the Rapsodie project

The Rapsodie project was carried out under the direction of UR RAP (Unité de recherche - Réponses Adaptatives des Populations et Peuplements de Poissons aux Pressions de l'environnement), a research unit of IRD-Senegal (Institut de Recherche pour le Développement).

The RAP research unit's activities are focused on increasing our knowledge of the mechanisms and consequences of natural and anthropogenic pressures on disturbed and/or overexploited continental aquatic systems.

The aim of this project is to model fish population dynamics by integrating different forms of stress (fishing, pollution, drought) and multi-species interactions. This involves studying the adaptation processes of certain populations and their impact on the evolution of populations [Villeneuve, 2003].

To explore the parameters specific to populations, as well as those of the environment, the researchers carried out simulations based on a dedicated model, following various scenarios, with artificial modifications to the parameters of the various components of the environment. In this project, population modeling is based on the individuals that make it up, using the individual-centered modeling method [Ginot et al. 2002], which respects two essential principles of biology:

- The uniqueness of each individual lies in the combination of his or her genetic heritage and the influences of his or her environment. An organism's physiology and behavior are closely linked to this combination.

- The principle of localization, which stipulates that an organism is primarily affected only by those organisms in its spatio-temporal vicinity.

To implement this project, the multi-agent approach was used, with Cormas as the multi-agent modeling platform. Cormas is based on the VisualWorks programming environment, which uses the Smalltalk programming language. It enables rapid simulation model development by describing coordinations between individuals and groups exploiting common resources. A brief presentation of these tools will follow, as we have already done with multi-agent systems.

4-2 Assessment of the Rapsodie project

The Rapsodie project model makes it possible to track the evolution of a fish population in space and time.
It includes a simulation interface and a visualization interface for simulated processes. It is, however, important to point out that the model could only be partially validated.

As mentioned above, this model reveals a number of constraints linked to the choice of development tools used. The slowness of the simulation and the rapid saturation of RAM (Random Access Memory) make it impossible to work with complex populations and large numbers of individuals. Nevertheless, Cormas is an excellent tool for prototyping, but from an "operative" point of view, its very design (space management and scheduling) requires a homogeneous distribution of simulated processes. This distribution is assumed to be equivalent, since it must be carried out on a regular spatial mesh. If these conditions are not met, there is a high risk of combinatorial explosion.

The first reaction to the above comments was to question the choice of Cormas and its Smalltalk programming language. It should be noted that another model was developed in Java by Nicolas DENFELD, based on Rapsodie. The latter did not give satisfaction, as RAM saturation was found, as with Cormas, at around 20,000 individuals, without calculating data extraction from the point of view of memory occupancy, which is a considerable handicap in relation to the modeling of a settlement.

4-3 Introducing Cormas and Smalltalk

4-3-1 Cormas

Cormas (common-pool Resources and Multi-Agent Systems) is a multi-agent simulation platform developed by the Green team at CIRAD (Centre de Coopération Internationale en Recherche Agronomique pour le Développement). This tool can be used to create a wide variety of multi-agent models. It is based on the VisualWorks development environment, which uses Smalltalk as its programming language, and offers a set of predefined classes and methods enabling it to build models without too much difficulty.

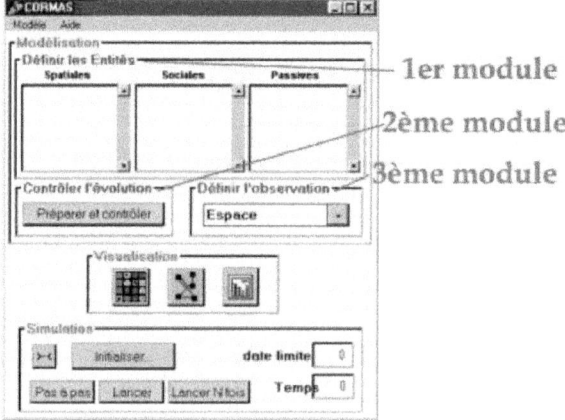

Figure 2: Cormas interface

The Cormas development platform is structured in the form of modules as shown in the diagram above:
- The first module concerns modeling, i.e. the definition of model entities called computer agents and their interactions. These interactions are symbolized by direct communication procedures (sending messages), and/or by sharing the same spatial medium. Three categories of entities are proposed:
    - spatial entities that symbolize the environment.
    - Social entities or agents.
    - Passive entities defined as opposed to social entities.
- The second module concerns simulation itself:
    - simulation space parameters (size, etc.).
    - scheduling of different events by time step.
    - launch the simulation.
- The third and final module allows you to define an observation of the dynamics and monitor the evolution of the model.

4-3-2 Smalltalk

Smalltalk is an object-oriented programming language that is an implementation method in which programs are organized as cooperating sets of objects, each representing an instance of a certain class, and all classes are members of a class hierarchy unified by inheritance relationships (see Appendix A).

Smalltalk offers a highly interactive development environment, and the use of abstraction and modularity in programs facilitates extensive reuse of previously developed programs and code elements. The VisualWorks development environment will be used to write Smalltalk code, visualize objects, fine-tune programs and develop applications.

All classes are directly accessible in the development environment and can therefore be redefined.

The features of smalltalk are as follows:
- In smalltalk, every element is an object.
- Every object is an instance of a class by definition of an object-oriented programming language.
- In smalltalk, the control structure is message sending.

5 Erlang's choice

In this section, we justify the choice of Erlang for the development of this model by explaining some of its features.

5-1 Introducing Erlang

The erlang language was developed in Sweden at Ericsson's CSLAB (Computer Science laboratory). This laboratory specializes in the design of telecommunications systems. In fact, it sounds like a contraction of "Ericsson Language".

Erlang is both a language and a development environment. It is the result of a combination of two programming styles: the concurrent approach and the declarative approach [Amstrong et al. 1996] and [Dacker, 2000]. Inspired by a declarative approach, this language originally worked within a prolog interpreter, being developed initially as an extension of the latter.

The Erlang development environment (virtual machine, compiler and applications) is completely open source, with new versions available (see Appendix B). The open-source nature of Erlang encourages a certain dynamism in the language. We have important tools such as the code editor and debugger that make application development easier. Erlang also features a Shell for launching commands interactively (see diagram 3 and Appendix B).

The technical characteristics and the way in which this language has been designed offer the Erlang environment undeniable advantages, both for developers and for users, who benefit from more stable and robust applications [Rémond, 2003]. Let's take a look at some of these features.

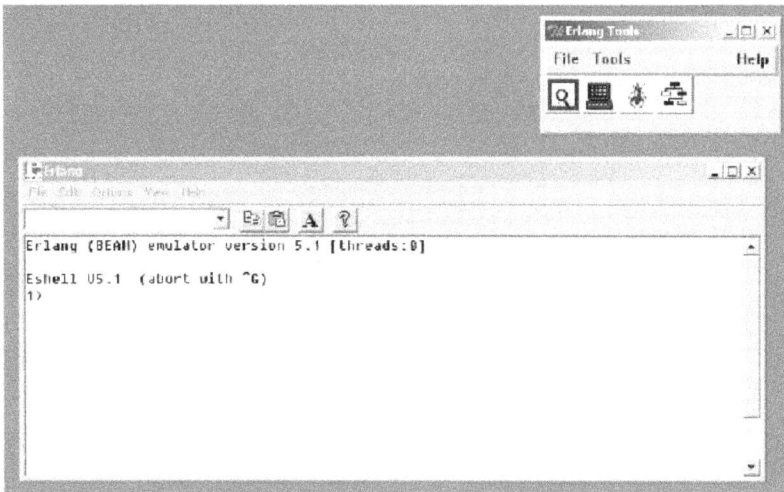
Diagram 3: Shell Erlang

5-1-1 Process management

Erlang has the particularity of managing lightweight processes (230 kB) with dynamically changing memory occupancy [Nystrom and Johnson, 2002]. Erlang processes communicate asynchronously by sending messages. The Erlang virtual machine is capable of handling a very large number of processes, and we will try to illustrate this with the proposed model.

Process management and system concurrency remain independent of the operating system, guaranteeing application portability.

5-1-2 The distributed environment

Erlang is designed to operate in a distributed environment. The environment is organized in nodes, and an Erlang node is represented by an Erlang virtual machine (often one node per processor). The Erlang virtual machine is able to create processes on other nodes running on different operating systems. These processes operate as if they were located on the same machine. The model proposed in this course is a distributed one. Application distribution mechanisms will be described in detail later.

5-1-3 Troubleshooting

The emergence of concepts such as supervision is the result of the separation between the code containing the application logic and the code in charge of error management. The code in charge of the application logic is under the control of the supervision code to manage any failures. Supervision can take place at several levels, with one process taking charge of supervising other processes, even if these are running on other nodes.

Another concept, called code migration, consists of configuring a process in a distributed system in such a way that if it has an execution problem on its node, it can run on another node and return to its original node once the problem has been solved. This feature ensures continuity of service even in the event of errors that are not known in advance.

5-1-4 Updating code

The system must be available at all times, given its use in the telecoms sector, where applications are used 24 hours a day, hence the need to reduce maintenance periods. With Erlang, it is possible to update application code without interrupting services.

5-1-5 Memory management

The Erlang development environment takes care of memory management, so the developer doesn't have to. Memory is allocated dynamically as required, and released when the memory spaces concerned are no longer in use. The system uses the garbage collection mechanism to handle these types of problems.

5-1-6 Productivity

The combination of all these features enables faster, more reliable application development, while avoiding the safety problems associated with variable overruns.

Erlang is well-suited to rapid development in the mock-up phase. With this approach, the development cycle is very short, based on a rapid sequence of development, integration and testing phases. Erlang can be used to develop real-time systems (software requiring response times of a few milliseconds).

5-1-7 Portability

Erlang code that has already been compiled (pseudo-code produced in a ".beam" file extension) can be executed by the virtual machine on any platform. Erlang code development does not need to take into account the particularities of the virtual machine on a given platform, which will facilitate code execution and distribution on networked machines.

5-1-8 Erlang principles and basics

Erlang programs must be structured around the notion of process, not object. As Erlang is defined as a concurrency-oriented language, it is very common to use programs (or processes) in parallel to solve a given problem. In addition to concurrency, development in Erlang involves other notions that need to be understood in order to better understand the Erlang philosophy. There are four such notions:

- **Functions** : A function is a sequence of one or more expressions, in the arithmetical sense of the term. It is a kind of filter that accepts input parameters as a basis for its execution, and returns an output that represents the result of evaluating the last expression. They play a central role in the implementation of the language, as Erlang is a declarative or functional language. With Erlang, a function is always referenced by the name of the function and the name of the module containing it. The latter is implicit in some cases, but there's no doubt about its existence.
- **Recursion**: This development technique consists in calculating the result of a function by iterating over the same function with a predefined output condition. The application of recursion produces more readable and compact code, facilitates list traversal and the translation of arithmetic calculations, but its use is not limited to these cases.
Example:

facto(0) -> 1 ;
facto(N) -> N *facto(N-1).

- **Unique variable assignment**: Erlang variables are used to access the values represented by these symbols. With Erlang, a value assigned to a variable can no longer be changed: this mechanism is known as unique variable assignment. Unique variable assignment tends to limit the edge effects that occur when a function changes the state of the system. An assigned variable is said to be "bound", i.e. it can no longer be assigned another value. Once assigned, a variable is released as soon as the program no longer needs to maintain its value in memory, i.e. when the variable is out of range of the instructions being evaluated by the program. Two rules determine the scope of variables:

    *Variables assigned to a function only exist within that function, and are destroyed when the function ends.

    * Variables are no longer considered to be linked to the entry of a new function. With Erlang, we only have local variables, not global ones.

- **Pattern matching**: This mechanism allows you to assign values to unrelated variables and test matches between values.

5-1-9 The particularity of Erlang variables

Syntactically speaking, an Erlang variable always has an initial capital letter. A variable is characterized by its name, which can be associated with a value: this was covered in the previous section.

There is no variable declaration in Erlang, as the operation of linking the variable to a value allows it to be assigned a type at the same time. Since a variable cannot be changed before it is destroyed, it is not possible to change its type once it has been determined.

Erlang is a high-level language: memory management, which involves taking different types into account for optimization purposes, no longer rests with the programmer, but with the virtual machine, based on the values contained in the variables. This is why Erlang's elementary types are very few in number and not very restrictive.

5-2 Concurrent programming

Concurrent programming is the assembly of parallel processes on one or more nodes. Processes are executed sequentially within a process, and all processes are executed in parallel.

5-2-1 Processes

An Erlang process is defined as an instance that hosts sequentially executed processes. Processes are generated by function calls. They terminate once the generating functions have been executed, and disappear from the system.

It's possible to create processes with Erlang and start their execution using Erlang's built-in functions: spawn/3, spawn_link/3, spawn/4 and spawn_link/4. As we said at the start of this section, a process begins with a function call, and the parameters of the spawn/3 function are nothing more than the module of the function called, its name and the list of its parameters. The spawn/4 and spawn_link/4 functions are used to create processes on remote nodes.

These functions return the identifiers of the processes they have just created, and do not wait for the functions to finish executing before doing so. A process ID is a reference to that process and is used to address it, for example, by sending it a message. The distributive nature of Erlang means that processes can be created on remote nodes. With Erlang, message-sending processes are very well implemented even for processes residing on remote nodes. The function called within one of these primitives must be exported from the module where it is defined to avoid producing an error.

Syntax :
  spawn(nom_module, nom_fonction, [param_fonction]).
  Spawn(nom_du_noeud,nom_module,nom_fonction,[param_fonction]).

In the Erlang environment, the memory occupation of a new process is very low: just over 230 bytes. This figure increases as the process is processed. Thousands of processes can be created simultaneously in a small amount of memory. According to studies carried out by Ericsson Laboratories, an Erlang node can execute more than 32,768 processes. With certain launch parameters, this number can reach 262,144 processes.

5-2-2 Communication between processes

It would be interesting to find a way of communicating between processes within the same application. Erlang has only message passing as a means of coordinating and synchronizing processes. This is an asynchronous operation that consists of sending an expression to one or more processes.

Message passing is based on two operations: sending a message and receiving a message. Let's take a look at the principles and syntax of these two operations.

- sending a message: the syntax is as follows:

Pid ! Message.
{Pid, Noeud} ! Message.

Pid represents the identifier of the recipient process, which must be known. The second case illustrates the sending of a message to a process located in a remote node. It is possible to use the process name instead of the process identifier. To name an Erlang process, use the standard register/2 function, with the process name, which is an atom, and the Pid, which is the process identifier, as parameters. You can also retrieve a process identifier by knowing the process name, using the whereis/1 function.

- Receiving a message: the syntax is as follows:

Receive
    MessageType1 -> Traitement1 ;
    MessageType2 -> Traitement2 ;
    ...
    MessageTypek -> Traitementk
end.

To use a message sent by a process, the message must be received by the receiving process. The receive operation consists in selecting a message from the message queue of the receiving process. The message is selected by performing a pattern match on the first clause of the receive instruction, reviewing all messages in the process queue. If no match can be made, then the environment attempts to match the next clause of the receive instruction with the set of messages in the queue, and so on. This procedure is illustrated in the diagram below.

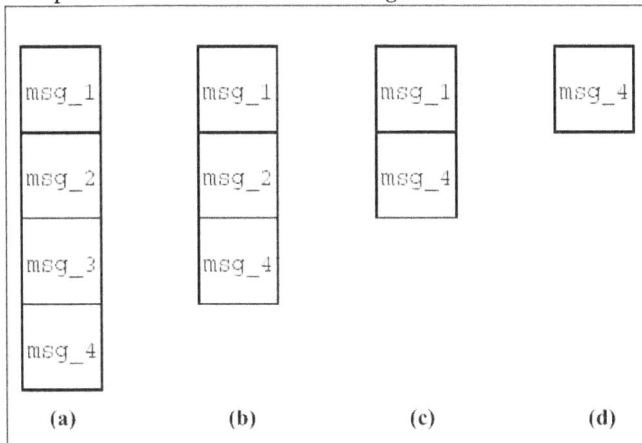

Consider the following receive instruction from a given process:
The inbox of the receiving process is shown below with the various pattern matching steps (diagram 4).

```
receive
    msg_3 -> Traitement3 ;
    msg_2 -> Traitement2 ;
    msg_1 -> Traitement1 ;
    ......................................
end.
```

Figure 4: Process inbox

5-3 Erlang, a distributed system

The Erlang language is designed to work in a distributed environment, so distribution remains one of Erlang's key features. There are many reasons to develop distributed applications using Erlang. We are going to list just a few of them:
- The ability to subdivide an application into several parts and evaluate them in parallel on different nodes. For example, create a real-time system, made up of several nodes, where jobs will be assigned to different nodes to reduce system response time.
- Cooperation between several nodes, so that the failure of one node does not penalize

the whole system.
- Access to resources is not tied to the operating system. A machine running Windows is able to run applications on a remote node running Unix.
- Scalability is also important: if the system is too slow, you can improve its performance by increasing the number of nodes (one processor per node), for example.

5-3-1 An Erlang node

An Erlang distributed system is a network of nodes. An Erlang node represents a virtual machine. From an Erlang node, you can create processes on other nodes, some of which may run on different operating systems, as described above. By default, an Erlang node is isolated. To initiate communication, it must belong to a set of Erlang nodes, have a process known as *net_kernel* that handles connection management and a port that enables it to communicate with other nodes on the network.

In a network, it's essential to be able to identify a node. By default, an Erlang node will have the name "*nonode@nohost*"; for it to function in a network, it needs a unique name. The name of a node is made up of two parts separated by the "@" character. The part after the "@" character is the network name of the machine where the node resides, guaranteeing the uniqueness of the node's name in the network. The other part identifies the node on the local machine, as it is possible to have several nodes on the same machine.

Node name consistency within a single machine is ensured by the *EPMD (Erlang Port Mapper Deamon)* system process. It records the names of all nodes that have been launched on this machine. Each node in a network is associated with a term known as "*cookie magic*", an atom (a constant containing information in the form of a sequence of characters) that enables a node to communicate with other nodes. A certain degree of security is provided by this "*cookie*" mechanism. For distribution, each node needs to know its neighbors in order to communicate with them. These *cookies* essentially function as passwords.

For two processes located on different nodes to communicate, the friendship between these two nodes must be declared by the *net_kernel* system processes of both nodes. In concrete terms, the *net_kernel* process of one node opens a port for that of the other node and associates this port with the table of atoms that can access it. This concept of friendship is a symmetrical property at process level. So, to end this friendship, simply issue the *erlang:disconnect_node/i* command by one of the processes residing on one of the nodes, with the name of the other node as the argument.

5-3-2 Erlang node properties

The launch of a node is accompanied by the determination of its properties. There are dynamic properties, which change over time, and static properties, which remain unchanged over time: they are closely linked to the node's behavior.

Static properties: There are only four of these properties, which are assigned values when the system is launched.
- *name*: This atom symbolizes the name of the machine and corresponds to *nonode@nohost* for an isolated node. This name must be modified so that the node can belong to a distributed system. It is accessed with the *node()* command.
- *communicating*: This is a Boolean atom, its value is *false* if the node is isolated, otherwise it is *true*. If the node becomes communicating, the atom's value is changed to true, after which it can no longer be changed. Use the *erlang:is_alive()* command to find out its value.

- *creation*: This non-negative integer is used to create a new reference, PID or Port, and to distinguish between different instances of the node. It is obtained from the *EPMD* process at system start-up.
- *preloaded*: This atom contains the list of modules that are preloaded at system startup and can be accessed with the *erlang:pre_loaded()* command.

Dynamic properties: These are properties that change with time. There are 16 of them, but we'll deal with the most important here.
- *atom_tables*: This is a table containing information about the node's friends. Each line is assigned to a friend and contains its name, a key and an empty atom table. A friend's line is automatically deleted as soon as the friendship between the two nodes is suspended.
- *I'riends*: this atom contains the names of friendly nodes, and is modified as soon as

a friendship with a new node is established. At the same time, it symbolizes the nodes authorized to connect to it. The *nodes()* command returns the atom's value.
- *magic_cookie*: This atom must be known by any process on a given node that wishes to communicate with a process residing on the current node. Its value can be known with the *erlang :get_cookie()* command and can be modified with the *erlang :set_cookie/2* command.
- *magic_cookies*: This is an atom like the previous one, but contains cookies from other nodes. These cookies cannot be accessed directly, but their value can be modified on the local node.
- *ports:* This atom contains the ports open on the node. Its value is implicitly modified if a new port is opened or if there is one less. The *erlang :ports()* command returns its value.
- *processes*: This contains the PIDs of processes that have been launched on this node and have not yet finished execution. Its value is modified when a new process is launched or at the end of a process's execution, and can be accessed with the_processes() command.

5-3-3 Distribution mechanisms

The node is the central element in an Erlang distributed system. The integration of a node into a distributed system is symbolized by the launch of a special process called *net_kernel*. Once this process has been launched, the node is given a name that is unique throughout the network. This simple operation of naming an Erlang runtime system transforms it into a distributed system.

TCP/IP sockets are used to enable remote nodes to communicate with each other. Let's take a look at the most commonly used commands in a distributed system.
- *erlang :disconnect_node(Node)* : forces disconnection of argument node at current node.
- *erlang :get_cookie()* : returns the *cookie magic* of the current node.
- *is_alive()*: returns true if the *net_kernel* is launched and false otherwise.
- *erlang :set_cookie(Node, Cookie)* : modifies the *cookie magic* of the node in argument, and this cookie will be used by the current node to connect to it. If the current node is passed as a parameter, the new cookie will be used by other nodes to connect to the current node.

- *nodes()*: returns the list of nodes that can access the current node.
- *node()*: returns the name of the current node.
- *monitor_node(Node, true[false):* allows the current node to monitor the status of the argument node. The *{nodedown, Node}* message is sent to it if the argument node disconnects.
- *spawn\spawn_link(Node, Module, function, args_function)*: creates a process on the remote node to execute the function.

The following flags are used when launching the *erl* or *werl* executable:
- *-name*: assigns a name to the current node.
- *-sname*: gives the current node a short name.
- *-hidden*: makes a node invisible.
- *-setcookie Cookie*: assigns a cookie to the current node, identical to the *erlang* command *:set_cookie(node(), Cookie)*.

The modules most commonly used to administer a distributed system are :
- *net_kernel*: the *net_kernel* is a system process launched on a communicating node. It implements the *spawn/4* and *spawn_link/4* functions, and provides authentication and network monitoring. The module of the same name enables dialogue with this process and contains a number of functions. Let's take a look at some of these functions:
  - *net_kernel:start()*: launches the *net_kernel* process, automatically if network parameters are enabled.
  - *net_kernel:allow(Node_list)*: this function limits access to the current node. The node that evaluates this function can only be accessed by the nodes listed in the *Node_list* variable. Any access attempt other than those specified will be refused.
  - *net_kernel:monitor_nodes(true\false)* : The process that evaluates this function receives copies of the *{nodeup, Node}* and *{nodedown, Node}* messages from the *net_kernel* process, which receives them from the runtime system.
- *net_adm*: this module contains several utilities for administering a network of Erlang nodes.
  - *net_adm:localhost()*: this command returns the name of the local host.
  - *net_adm:ping(Node)*: allows the current node to test the connection with the

node in parameter. It returns *pong* if the connection works *and pang* if it doesn't.
- *net_adm:word()*: this function launches the *EPMD* process on all workstations specified in the *.hosts.erlang* file and *pings* all nodes residing on these workstations. If successful, the connection is created on all nodes running on the specified workstations.

- *auth*: this module name also refers to a server or process that determines which nodes are authorized to communicate in an Erlang node network. Every message sent is accompanied by the *cookie magic* of the receiving node. When a message is received by a node, the system looks at the *cookie magic* accompanying the message. If not, the message is transformed into a *badcookie message* and sent to the *net_kernel* system process. By default, the *net_kernel* sends the message back to the *auth* system process, which will then take the appropriate action for unauthorized messages. Let's take a look at some of the functions of the *auth* module:
    - *auth :is_auth(Node)*: finds out whether the connection to this node given in parameter is authorized and returns *yes* if it is, *no* if the node doesn't exist or if the connection is not authorized.

auth:exists(Node): this function tests the existence of the node passed in parameter. It returns *yes* if the node exists and *no* otherwise.

5-3-4 Connection

In the previous section, we discussed the connection mechanisms between Erlang nodes. Evaluation of the *nodes() command,* after launching a node, returns an empty list: this means that, when the system is started, the node has no information about the existence of other nodes in the network. An attempt to connect two nodes is only made when commands such as :
- *spawn(Node, Module, Function,Argument).*
- *net_adm :ping(Node).*

If the connection is authorized after the execution of one of these commands, the current node is now able to know its friends. Evaluating the *nodes()* command returns a list of nodes that are allowed to connect and have attempted to do so at least once. These multiple aspects of Erlang lead us to use this language to implement our model.

5-4 Comparison between Erlang and C++

In this section, we'll try to justify our choice of Erlang over other programming languages such as C++. C++ is one of the most widely used programming languages today. It's an object-oriented language and the basis of many software applications. Erlang is part of this new generation of development languages. It is quite different from C++, mainly because it employs a programming style called functional programming and offers built-in concurrency. In this section, we will evaluate Erlang and compare it to C++, based on a study carried out by an Ericsson laboratory [Grasftrom andAronsson, 1995].

To compare these two languages, a set of small test programs were made in C++ and Erlang. In the study report, they also spread out the experiments and test results that were obtained.

First, we'll give a brief introduction to the C++ language, and then move on to the comparison itself, by talking about a few aspects of Erlang.

5-4-1 The C++ language

C++ is an object-oriented programming language. It was developed in the 80s at Bell Labs by a team led by Bjarne Stroustrup. Initially, it was a small extension of the C language for a research project in the field of object-oriented programming. The aim of the design was that the language should be efficient, portable and improve on C's data types.
C++ should be compatible with C. Indeed, it's impossible to present C++ without starting with some of the properties of C.

In C, variables are entities where data can be stored and modified. Most languages make a distinction between different types of data, e.g. a number is not the same as a letter and so on. A C programmer needs to define the data types to be stored in each variable. The language recognizes only the function structure. A program written in C is a set of functions, each of which can call itself and the others. There are so many features of the C language that deserve to be explained, but we'll move straight on to those of C++, which is the subject of this section.

References are implicitly used in function calls and there's no way of telling whether a parameter is passed as a value or a reference just by looking at the function call and not the operator used. Classes are structures in C++ that operate like functions on data. Classes and objects are very important concepts in C++. Objects are defined as instances of classes.

The main aim with C++ was to include objects in C programming. In this style of programming, everything is built around objects. Objects communicate via messages, which are handled by methods implemented by their corresponding classes.

5-4-2 Comparison programs

Four test programs were produced by this team of researchers to enable a meaningful comparison to be made between these two languages. Two versions of each program were made, one in Erlang and one in C++. The problems were oriented towards different sectors:
1- **Four in a row**: a simple game that requires a large search tree, a large volume of data and long calculations.
2- **Nranax**: a number analyzer, a process typically used in the telecommunications sector.
3- **Spreadsheet**: an engine that requires the evaluation and analysis of expressions.
4- **Runge-Kutta**: a numerical algorithm for solving differential equations using iterative calculation methods.

5-4-3 Comparison results

In this section, we'll show you the results of coding the four problems listed above.

	Time/ C++	Number of line/ C++	Time /Erlang	Number of lines/ Erlang
Nranax	11:30h	557	2 :20h	172
Spreadsheet	40h	1416	10h	392
Four in a row	18h	608	9 :45h	363

Runge-Kutta	0 :3Oh	52	0 :3Oh	31	

Figure 5: Comparison test results

Measurements are made on the size of the code, reasonably on the number of lines, and the time taken for coding. This is due to the very high level of optimization in both languages, which is of some relevance to the results. In some cases, execution speed will also be measured. Because of the complexity of these problems, they have chosen to write separate programs and then assemble them. The aim is that the estimated time should be the time taken exclusively for coding.

Given the numbers presented in the table above, we can say that programming in Erlang is on average 3 times faster and 3 times less voluminous in terms of lines of code than in C++. It should be pointed out that an Erlang program contains many more comments than a C++ program, and these comments form part of the code count. It should also be noted that Erlang processes will be used if this is a large project, which could create concurrency errors to some extent. However, it would be very difficult to find complex memory management errors in C++. Code reuse considerably reduces coding time. Since this applies to both languages, it should not have a major influence on results.

The use of processes is recommended in Erlang documentation. Processes also simplify I/O handling. Another reason for using processes is that Erlang lacks other ways of subtracting data. The use of processes in a functional language naturally presents some obstacles, especially in inter-process communication. Bottlenecks are the type of error often encountered when using processes in C++. They are very common in real-time systems. With regard to these potential problems, the structure of a program in Erlang would differ greatly from that of a program in C++.

5-4-4 Study conclusions

Data type manipulation differs in the two languages. Erlang has dynamic data types, which are only checked at runtime. Unlike C++, where data types are static and checked at compile time. Polymorphism is possible in C++ using templates (mechanisms for generating functions and classes based on parameter types), and the same results are obtained with

Erlang thanks to its dynamic typing. Concurrent programming, with processes and interprocess messages, is the basic concept in Erlang. Automatic memory allocation and deallocation, with the garbage collection mechanism, are standard features in a language like Erlang, which has no destructive updates.

Erlang's performance, in terms of speed of execution, is due to the implementation of inter-process communication, i.e. message sending and error handling. For example, if a pattern-matching error occurs in a process, causing it to stop, a message is sent to all processes linked to it. With C++, the program is exposed to these undiscovered errors at compile time, which can cause the program to crash. Modularity is achieved by objects at all levels in C++. In Erlang, processes are used at a higher level of modularity and functions at a lower level. Memory management, pattern matching and recursion are features that free the programmer from many tedious tasks. The functionalities achieved with small objects in C++ are achieved in parallel by functions in Erlang. The simplicity and low cost (memory occupation and CPU time) offered by Erlang for the implementation of large programs such as servers are not obtained with C++. This type of program, in terms of cost for object-oriented programming, is very high.

6 Model description

We will show that Erlang is an appropriate language for multi-agent simulation, as it already offers integrated functionalities and mechanisms adapted to the development of this type of application [Arthursson et al. 1996]. These include concurrency management, asynchronous communication between processes and distribution, plus the system's excellent availability and real-time aspect. A multi-agent application may require a certain degree of security for communication between agents. Part of this security is managed by a protocol that authenticates the recipient when a message is sent. The asynchronous communication implemented in Erlang facilitates greater process autonomy. For example, waiting for an acknowledgement of receipt when sending a message can cause the application to freeze.

6-1 Model architecture

We propose a system composed of nodes and agents. The different nodes represent the different zones of the environment. A typology of agents is defined according to two categories: biological agents and organizational agents. This categorization is linked to the activities or roles assigned to them.

Biological agents are agents that have certain biological characteristics in relation to the model representation. These biological characteristics can be summarized as their ability to move, survive, grow, reproduce and die.

On each node, there are several organizational agents who cooperate with each other and with other agents to achieve a more stable (evolution of the number of individuals as a function of time) and more dynamic system. These agents can communicate with system processes to request services or gather information. Organizational agents are: the list manager (e.g. lists of male and female biological agents), the transfer manager, the transfer coordinator and the statistics manager, who is responsible for taking measurements. The organization of a node is shown in diagram 6, with the various interactions between agents.

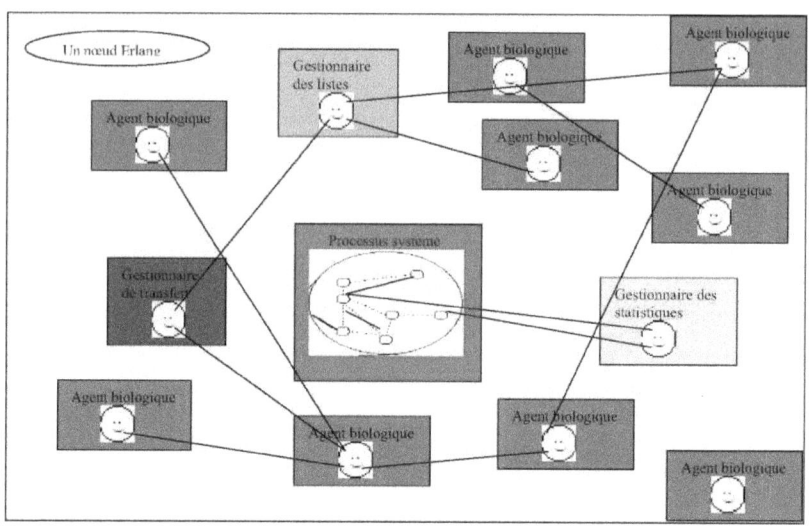

Node organization diagram 6

6-1-1 Organizational agents

These agents are unique in their kind. They are, of course, not mobile, since they are associated with each node and because of their roles as stabilizer, coordinator and informant. This structuring provides greater visibility of the model's reproduction, displacement and stability processes.

The level of modularity obtained with this organization allows a certain degree of cooperation between agents to carry out complex tasks. It is interesting to consider the particularities of Erlang when developing this type of application. The way in which Erlang process inboxes are managed, for example, means that we have to lighten up the correspondence tests to achieve faster processing (see section 5-2-2).

- The transfer coordinator exists only on the central node. This central node differs from the other nodes only in that the application is launched from this node, and this is where the transfer coordinator is located. This agent has information on neighboring nodes (memory occupancy, processor occupancy, etc.) via the transfer manager. This information is updated cyclically. It synchronizes the activities of the transfer managers on the various nodes. The rule defined for transfers is as follows:

the node with the heaviest load transfers some of its people to the node with the lightest load. If the coordinator decides which node is to make transfers, it will inform the transfer manager of the given node.

- The transfer manager informs the coordinator of the node's status on request, and triggers the movement of agents.

    (see diagram 7). The transfer manager takes the load off the processor by deciding whether or not to migrate fish based on the state of the node. If it needs to trigger a transfer, it asks the list manager for the list of male and female agents existing on the node. Once it has these lists, it selects an equal number of males and females to move. Warning messages are sent to agents who need to move.

- The role of the list manager is to store the identifiers of the male and female agents in the zone where he is located. These lists are updated if an individual dies or is born. This list manager plays a key role in facilitating dialogue between agents and ensuring system stability (see section 6-7).

- The statistics manager is a stationary agent which dialogues with system processes to gather certain information (see diagram 7). In this case, it memorizes the number of individuals in the zone in which it is located. Other information, such as transfer rate, memory space used and processor occupation, can also be managed by this agent.

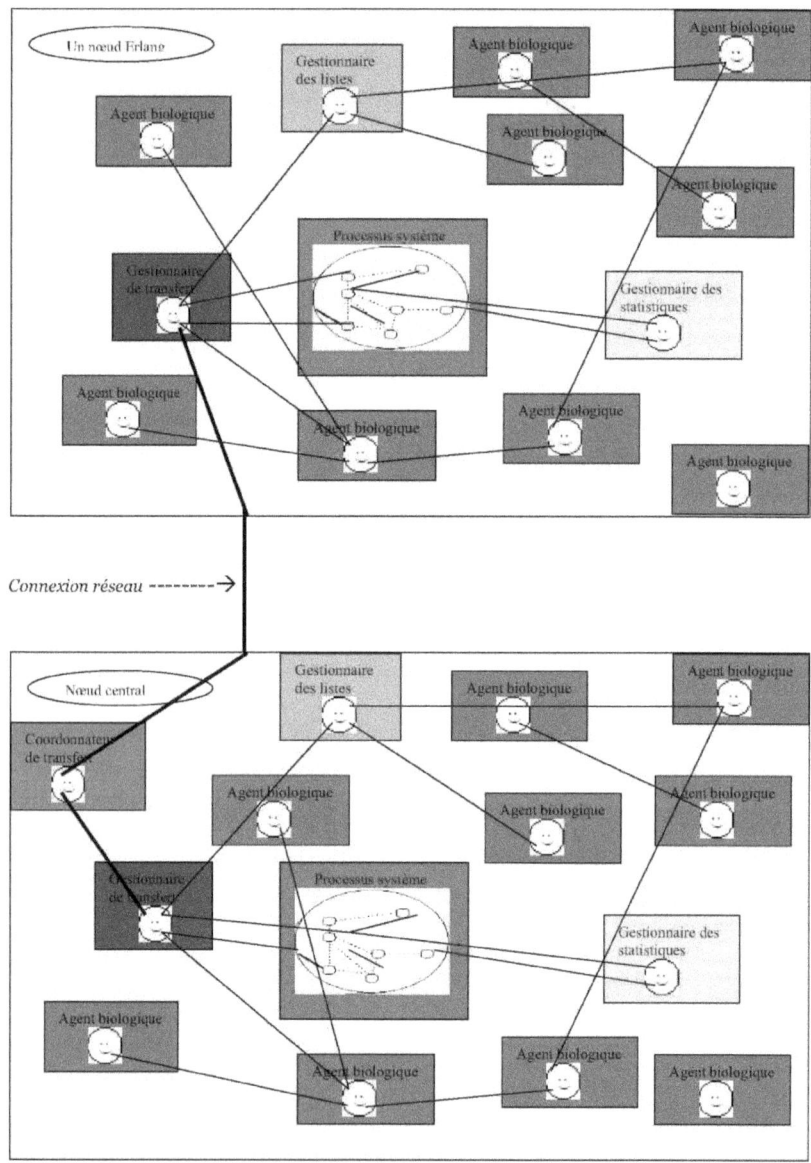

Diagram 7: communication between the central node and a given node

6-1-2 Biological agents

At the opposite end of the spectrum from organizational agents are the biological agents specific to the field of application. These agents represent the biological entities of the environment, their main characteristics being their ability to move, grow and reproduce, the three aspects we will attempt to illustrate in this model. A biological entity is either male or female.

- A male is an autonomous mobile agent. His autonomy is symbolized by the fact that he is the sole decision-maker when it comes to triggering his main activity, which is to reproduce. There is no control over this agent. It can communicate with other agents such as the list manager, the females and the transfer manager in its zone. It communicates with other agents either to breed or to move. To reproduce, he needs to communicate with the list manager and the female sent by the latter. A male is able to move from one node to another according to the resources of the zone - in this case, the loads of the current node. Synchronization with the transfer manager is required at a local level to carry out a move.
- The sex difference is between a male and a female. Apart from sex, these two types of agent have the same activities. The autonomy that characterizes males also applies to females. Sexual reproduction is represented in this model. For this activity, these two types of agent are highly complementary. We'll go into a little more detail in section 6-7.

6-2 Representing the environment

The medium is divided into several zones. Each zone is represented by an Erlang node, and all the nodes together make up the environment. In this model, we have not integrated any characteristics of the environment. However, it is possible to represent characteristics such as salinity, resources, multiple disturbances and so on. Our aim is first and foremost to be able to represent a very large number of biological agents (fish), and to be able to simulate the growth, reproduction, movement and death of these agents.

6-3 Representing an individual

A biological entity (fish) is represented by an Erlang process. Characteristics such as sex, age, size and number of offspring are represented. Updating these characteristics is facilitated by the computer structure (record) used to implement this type of data. This update is managed internally by the agent according to arbitrarily chosen rules. An individual has a limited lifespan, depending on its size and the number of descendants. It communicates with other individuals by sending messages. This correspondence is linked to the characteristics of Erlang, which is used as a programming language. Only natural death is represented. An individual is able to move from one zone to another. This representation of an individual fish by a single Erlang process is linked to its represented activity. An individual fish has little to do other than move and reproduce.

In a situation representing a slightly more complex activity, we could consider a set of Erlang processes to represent a biological entity (see diagram 8). These processes will perform specific tasks, such as communicating with other agents, coordinating reproduction, searching for food, moving around, etc. The approach is to encapsulate the agent in a closure. The approach is to encapsulate the agent in an agent closure. In this approach, we'll consider that an agent is made up of several Erlang processes, and that these processes run in the agent closure. The closure will be composed of several parts:

- First, there is a control agent or supervisor who is responsible for the agent, the processes serving the agent and controlling resource usage. At regular intervals, the agent supervisor checks how much resource is being used by the agent's processes. Resources include CPU usage and the amount of memory used by each agent. When an agent uses too many resources, the supervisor decides whether or not to stop it. With this approach, an agent can only use up a limited amount of resources, if it wants to survive long enough to complete its tasks. In this case, resources are system characteristics. It is possible to map resources to the environment, provided the properties of the environment are represented.
- It should be pointed out that an agent can have an agent dictionary, which serves as persistent memory for agent processes. All the information required for the agent's processes to function correctly will be found and stored in this dictionary.
- Finally, a part that will take care of communicating with other agents to accomplish certain tasks needs to be implemented.

All these parts must follow the agent as it moves between nodes. With this approach, modularity will be respected, but there is a drawback in that the agents will use a lot of system resources. Implementing everything in the form of processes is the normal way of designing such applications in Erlang, and the language will have a major influence on the basic architecture of the agents.

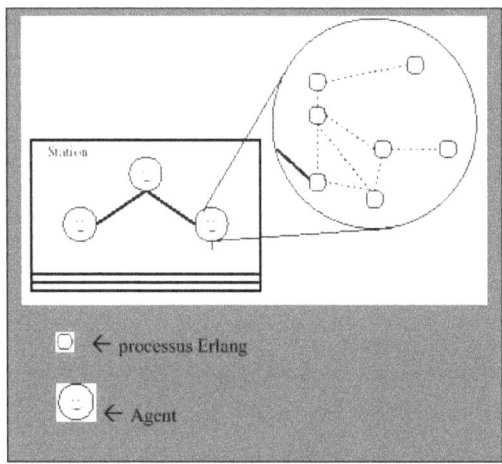

Figure 8: several Erlang processes per agent

6-4 Representation of biological functions

6-4-1 Growth

In this model, four characteristics of an individual have been represented: sex, age, height and number of offspring. The aim is to show that with Erlang, it is possible to represent this type of data and make it evolve over time. A structure called "record" is used to abstract this information. After X milliseconds, age and size are increased. The age is increased by one and the height by a randomly selected number less than the individual's age. This shows that it is possible to use more realistic equations such as Von BERTALANFY's to model the biological growth of an individual (Rapsodie project).

6-4-2 Moving

Our system is made up of several nodes. Agents are represented by Erlang processes. It should be pointed out that there is no direct way (an Erlang primitive) to move processes from one node to another. If a process "wants" to move, it must create a new process on the destination node and then terminate on the local node. The state of the old process is transferred by the arguments to the generated process. This method is used to model agent mobility. An individual's characteristics are not modified during a move. They are transferred to the newly generated agent.

The movement of an individual is linked to the state of the zone (node) in which it is located. The transfer manager assesses the state of the zone, and it's up to the transfer coordinator to decide which zone to lighten and which to populate. Once this decision has been made, the transfer manager of the chosen zone asks certain individuals in the zone to move.

6-4-3 Mortality

In this model, only natural death is represented. A maximum size and a minimum number of offspring are defined. The death of an individual is linked to these two constraints. The minimum number of offspring ensures a high number of individuals in the zone and control over this number. Each individual has total control over its number of offspring and its size. The management of these two characteristics is internal, but it is possible to have external management or influence on these characteristics in a more realistic model. For example, in Rapsodie, mortality is due to environmental conditions (e.g. salinity), i.e. an element external to the agent. Before exiting the system, the agent must inform the zone list manager so that the latter can update the lists of agent identifiers. Incidentally, this type of message has the highest priority in the list manager's inbox. This procedure enables the list manager to work with real values, and to a certain extent ensures system stability. This parameter should by no means be neglected, because if it's badly managed, it can put agents on hold indefinitely, waiting for responses from a non-existent agent.

6-4-4 Reproduction

In this model, an individual's main activity is to reproduce. Sexual reproduction is modeled, which necessarily implies synchronization between males and females who wish to reproduce. Both males and females can initiate reproduction. This initiative is symbolized by the request to the list manager for the identifier of an individual of the opposite sex. Once this identifier is known, if it's a female, a message asking her to breed is sent. If it's a male, the female sends him a message notifying him of her desire to reproduce. In both cases, an affirmative response is sent.

Reproduction is symbolized by the creation of a new individual. The probability of this being a male or a female is ¥2. The female rests for a few milliseconds after each reproduction. A reproducing female informs the reproducing male. She also sends a message to the list manager to update the lists of individuals in the zone. After each reproduction, both the male and the female increment the number of their offspring, and the individual created in turn seeks to reproduce.

6-5 Results

Tests are carried out based on this proposed model. A system consisting of three nodes is considered, and the load distribution is linked to the machine powers. Two Erlang nodes are used to store the processes (individuals) created. The third is used to launch the application and store the transfer coordinator. The latter is referred to as the central node, as described in section 6-1-1.

The tests carried out are presented in the form of curves to see and interpret the evolution of the number of individuals and processor occupation, in terms of percentage as a function of time on the two nodes, and to make comparisons if necessary. Four test cases are considered, varying the initial number of individuals:
- 200 individuals: with this small number, the phenomenon of reproduction and the death of individuals will be easier to understand.
- 40,000 individuals: this initial number of individuals will illustrate the speed of population evolution and the stability of the system with a greater or lesser number of individuals.
- 100,000 individuals: it's important to remember the objective underlying the development of such an application. With such an initial number of individuals, we will be able to project the system's behavior and predispositions, so as to be involved in the further development of this model in the future.
- 200,000 individuals: the limits of the system must be taken into account to avoid situations that could lead to system instability.

For each of these numbers initially taken, we'll present three curves: on the first, we'll represent the evolution of the number of individuals as a function of time on the two nodes (entitled Rox and Yassa Poulet with the same CPU performance (2.00 GHz-1.99 GHz), RAM (256)) and on the other two, we'll show the processor occupation as a function of time on each node.

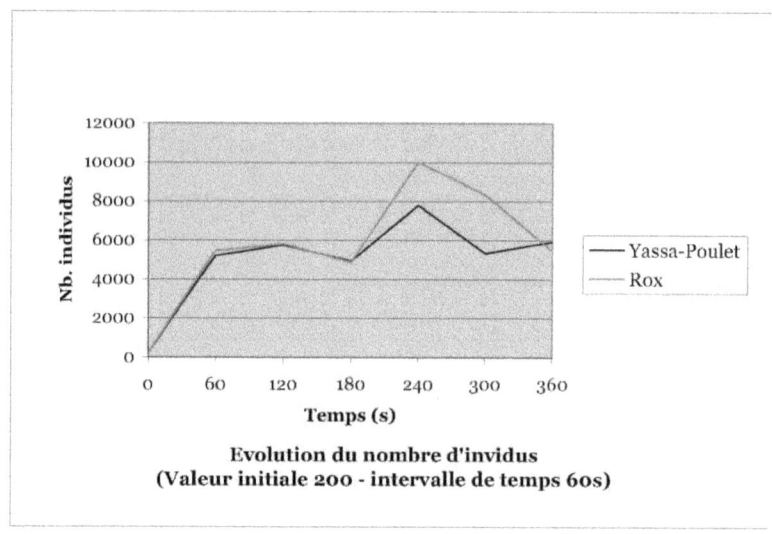

Diagram 9

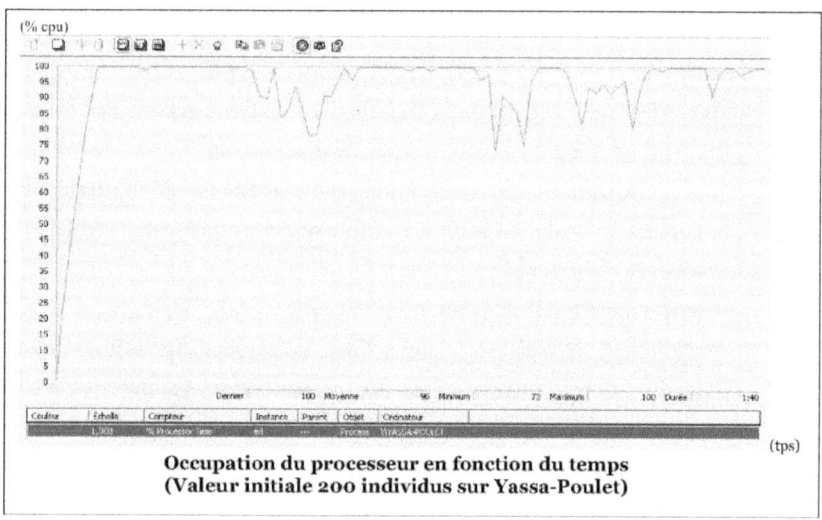

Diagram 10

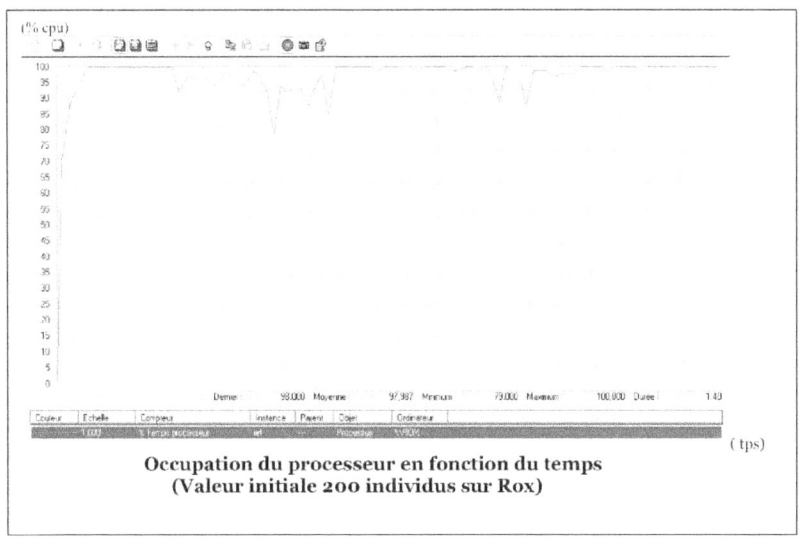

Diagram 11

In the four situations defined above (variation in the number of individuals), tests are carried out with the same number of males and females. Based on these initial results, the simulation is run initially with 200 males and 200 females. Figure 9 clearly shows that the evolution of the number of individuals is almost the same on both nodes. From a computational point of view, this can be interpreted as a certain stability of the application. The speed at which the population evolved is too important to mention. From an initial 200 individuals, we reached just over 5,000 after 60 seconds of simulation. This clearly illustrates the speed of the system and, from a biological point of view, the very high availability of individuals for reproduction and very rapid compensation for mortality. This speed is due to the full availability of both processors on both nodes. In terms of application execution, Yassa-Chicken averages 96% CPU time and Rox 97.98% (Figure 10 and Figure 11).

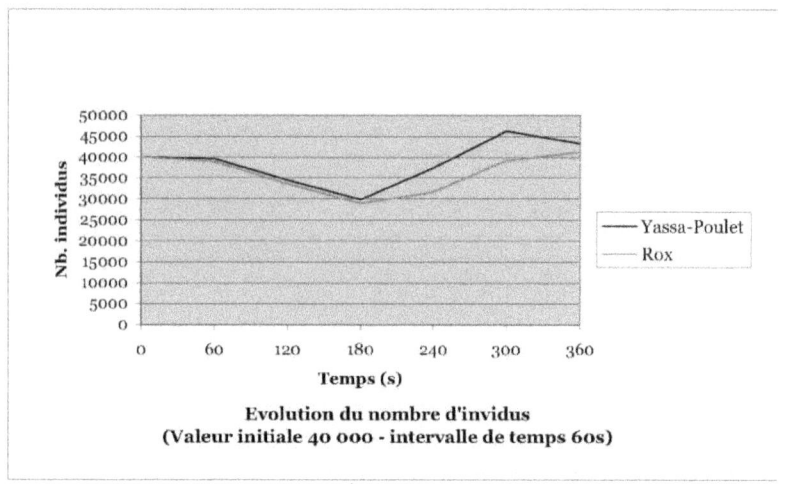

Diagram 12

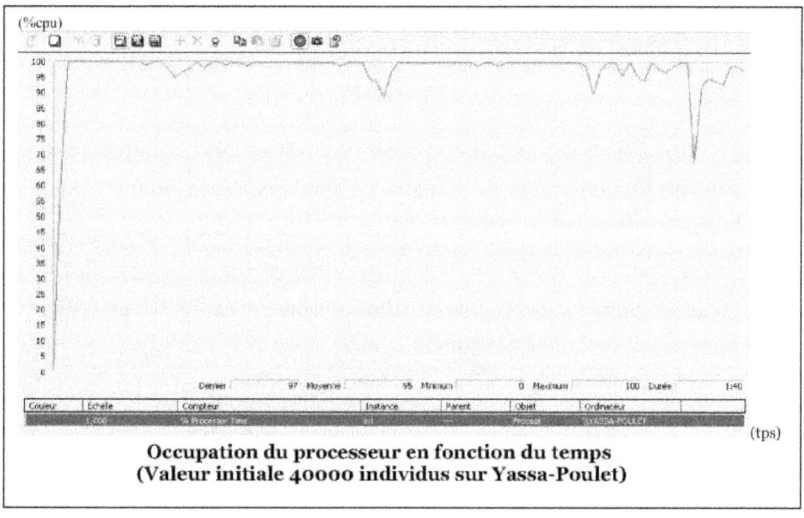

Diagram 13

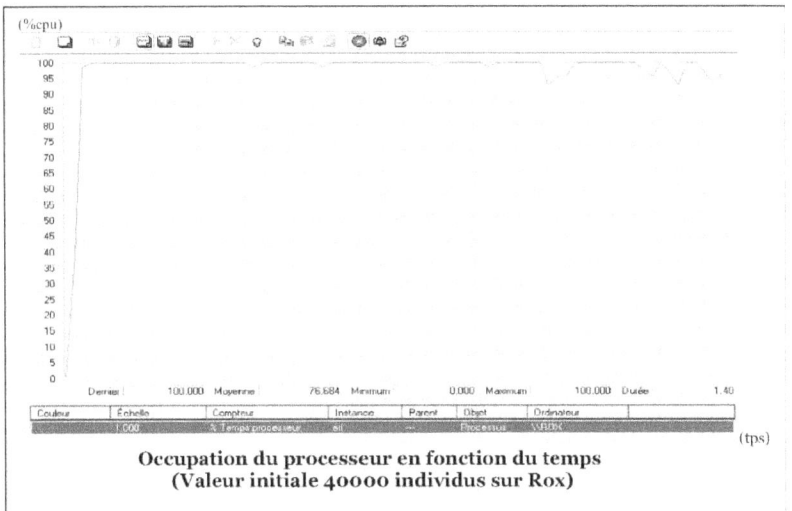

Occupation du processeur en fonction du temps
(Valeur initiale 40000 individus sur Rox)

Figure 14

If we recall the difficulties encountered with Rapsodie, with this relatively high initial number of individuals, we observe very good behavior of the model and the system in particular. With Rapsodie, the memory is saturated at around 20,000 individuals. Comparing this with the results already obtained, we can say that we have cleared at least one hurdle, as shown in diagram 12 (a more or less significant evolution in the number of individuals).

The biological characteristics considered and the mortality criteria played a major role in the variation in the number of individuals. Implicitly, this somewhat unrealistic evolution is due to the arbitrary choice of criteria used to represent certain biological functions. The two nodes occupy more processors, but this is far from being a problem for a system as powerful as Erlang.

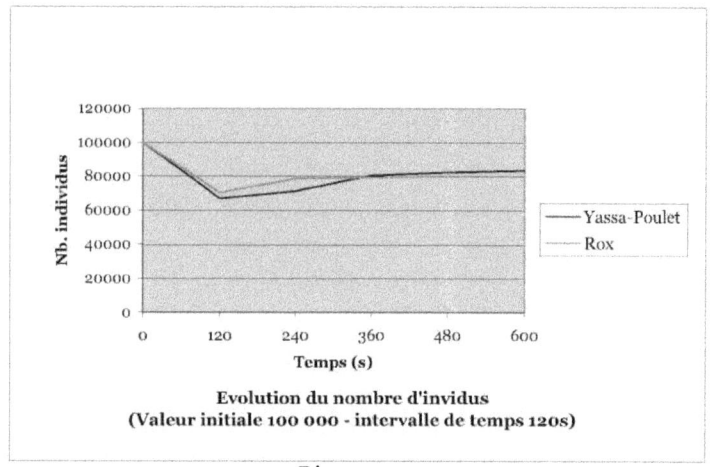

Diagram 15

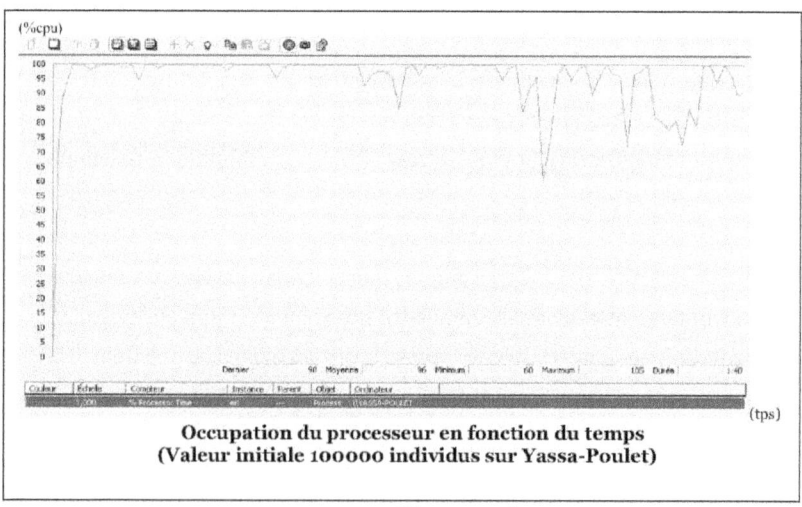

Diagram 16

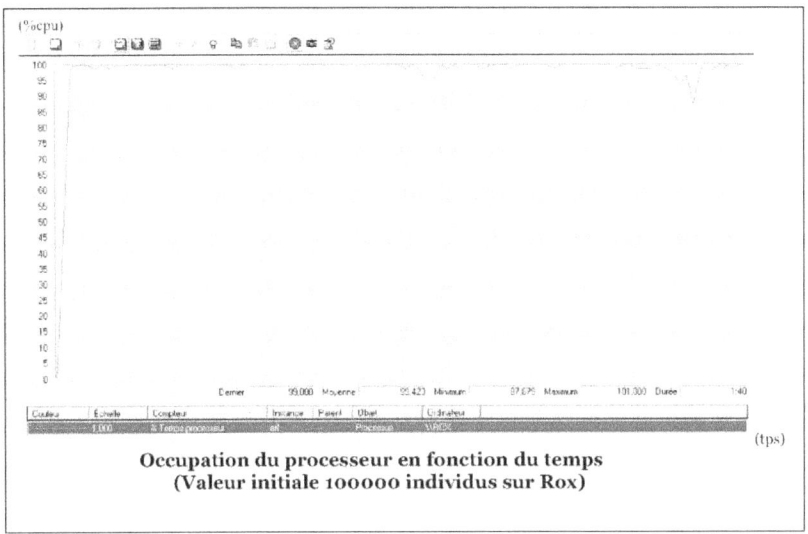

Diagram 17

With an initial number of 100,000 individuals in each zone, we can end up with impressive figures when considering a larger network of Erlang nodes. Even with this very high number of biological agents (individuals), we can see that communication between agents works "wonderfully", because at some point we observe a growth in both curves (diagram 15).

It is important to note that it would be very difficult to reach 100,000 individuals. We've seen a stabilization at around 80,000 individuals, and this number is quite satisfactory in relation to the objectives we had set ourselves. From this, it follows that there is a definite interest in taking this conceptual work further, as aspects have only been illustrated to highlight Erlang's predispositions for the development of this type of application. On the Rox node, the average processor occupancy is 99%, while on Yassa-Chicken it's 96% (diagrams 16 and 17). This is also linked to the architectures of the two computers.

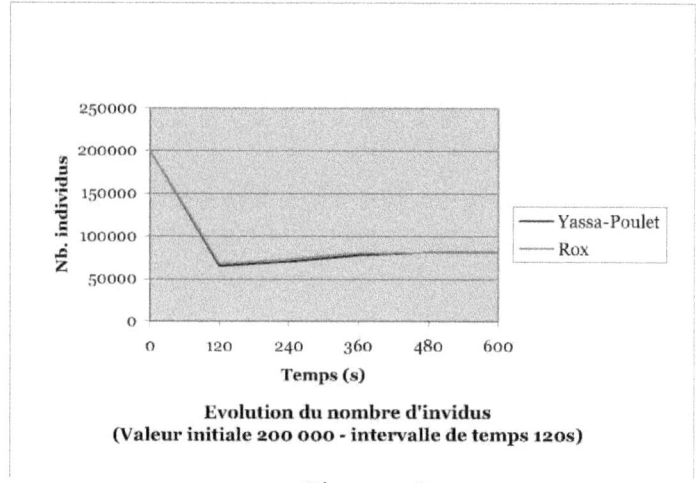

Evolution du nombre d'invidus
(Valeur initiale 200 000 - intervalle de temps 120s)

Diagram 18

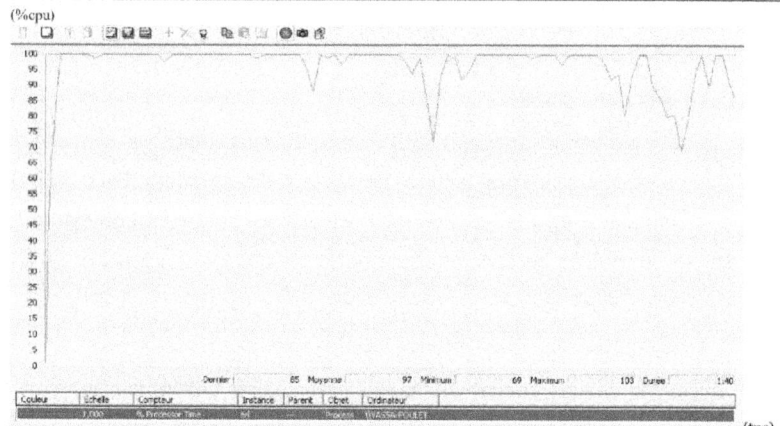

Occupation du processeur en fonction du temps
(Valeur initiale 200000 individus sur Yassa-Poulet)

Figure 19

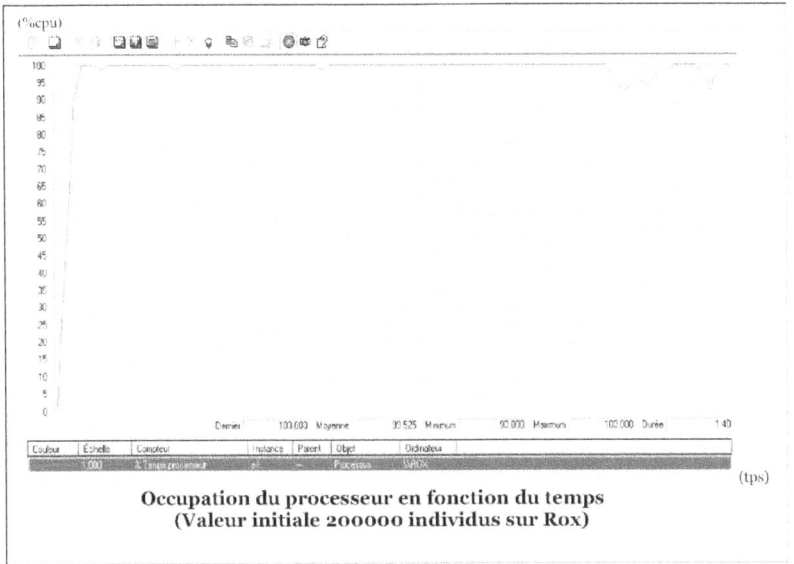

**Occupation du processeur en fonction du temps
(Valeur initiale 200000 individus sur Rox)**

Diagram 20

The study of this curve (diagram 18) provides information on the need to take into account the system's characteristics. Earlier in this brief, we set out the system's capabilities in terms of the number of processes it can handle: 262,144 is the maximum number of processes the system can handle. By launching 200,000 processes on each node, the system is forced to react to avoid disastrous consequences. As a result, the system reacted very quickly, with a clear decrease in both curves (diagram 18). Processor occupancy is very important, not for the proper functioning of the agents (Erlang processes) but for interacting with the system to lighten the processor (diagrams 19 and 20). Biological agents also suffer the same effects, as the reproduction phenomenon is not very visible, and the mortality of agents is very difficult to dissociate from the consequences of the system's reaction.

7 The outlook

The proposed model is very interesting, as it deploys a novel multi-agent simulation architecture in a concurrent process environment, and its use is well suited to fish population dynamics phenomena. Nevertheless, there are still aspects to be improved in this model, especially concerning the biological aspect with a better representation of biological characteristics and functions by considering, for example, more realistic growth criteria, as well as a representation of several species of biological agents. This work will be made possible through collaboration with IRD biologists and the reuse of equational forms modeling growth, combined with the application of mortality rates etc.

The representation of a biological agent by several Erlang processes proposed in section 6-3 could be considered in the future for better agentification. From a computational point of view, the distributed nature of Erlang has been used extensively to increase the number of agents and provide a better structuring of the environment. This could be improved by increasing the number of nodes (one processor per node).

The coupling of such a model with a database seems interesting, especially as Erlang has a very powerful DBMS called Mnesia. Data management in a telecoms system requires a high degree of error tolerance and consistency in the DBMS (database management system). This DBMS can be considered object-relational, and these tables can be distributed over a heterogeneous network. Such a coupling may slow down the simulation, but in another sense may help to lighten the load on the processors that need it, according to the results presented in section 6-5.

Conclusion

The essential result of this work is a proposed conceptual model capable of implementing a complex system in a concurrent process environment (Erlang). It's no mean feat to have shown that Erlang is well suited to the development of this type of application. This model provides a general vision for the representation in Erlang of the environment, the biological individuals that make it up and the interactions between these individuals, as well as the phenomena that result from these interactions. As far as the representation of biological functions is concerned, Erlang provides important mechanisms for implementing this type of information.

Many of the questions raised by the Rapsodie project have been answered, notably the slowness of simulation, rapid saturation and, above all, the use of a very large number of individuals. Nevertheless, a great deal of work remains to be done, in particular to represent the characteristics of the environment with reproduction, growth and mortality phenomena closer to reality, with a view to obtaining a slightly more realistic model.

Appendix A
Smalltalk

i Development environment

We use the **visualworks** development environment to write smalltalk code, visualize objects, design programs and develop applications.
The system consists of three main parts:
- The virtual machine.
- The image file.
- Source files.

i-i the virtual machine

It comprises a processor, virtual processes and an assembly language (producing byte code). It ensures that the supplied smalltalk code functions correctly (it transforms the smalltalk code into byte code, which is then interpreted by the virtual processor).

1-2 The image file

It contains the byte code interpreted by the virtual machine, as well as the objects contained in the system at a given time.

1-3 Source files

A source file contains the textual code of the system's initial methods and the ".change" file for methods added by the developer.

2 Language syntax

2-1 Constants

We have the following constants: numbers, characters, strings, symbols and arrays.
- **Numbers :**
    5.12,   -5, etc.
- **Characters:** objects representing symbols of the alphabet.
    $a, $g , $v etc.
- **Character strings :**
    hello', 'world', etc.
- **Symbols:** objects representing character strings used for system names.
    # red, #+, etc.
- **Tables:** these represent data structures whose contents can be referenced by an integer from 1 to the size of the table. They respond to messages to access an element, modify an element, etc.
    #(12 5), #($a $b $c), #(('u' 'n') 'two' ($t $r $o $i $s)), etc.

2-2 Variables

A variable is an object. There are private variables, accessible only to a single object, and shared variables, accessible to several objects.
- The name of a variable begins with a lowercase letter for private (local) variables and an uppercase letter for shared (global) variables.
    a, index, Rectangle, etc...
- An object's data is stored in variables called instance variables, which represent the object's current state. The contents of these variables can only be accessed by one of the

object's methods.
- Assignment allows you to change the contents of a variable.
  index:= 3
  index := index - 1
- A pseudo-variable refers to an object that cannot be modified by assignment.
  nil, true, false, self, etc.

2-3 Messages

A message is a request to an object (receiver) to execute one of these methods. Smalltalk expressions are interpreted as sending a message. Objects interact by sending messages. There are three types of message.
- Unary messages :
  Are those sent to an object with no parameters, only the receiver is concerned.
  Exple : x sin.
- Binary messages :
  They correspond to a method, an argument.
  Exple : index - 1
- Keyword message:
  They allow you to construct messages with as many arguments as you like (each keyword ends with a ":").
  Exple : #('a','b','c') at : 1 put : 'b'.

- Priority
The assessment begins with :
1- Evaluating unary expressions .
2- Evaluation of binary expressions.
3- Finally, the evaluation of keyword messages.

- sequence and cascade
A sequence is a series of messages sent to various objects. In smalltalk, two instructions are separated by a "." .

Cascading consists in sending several messages to the same object, separated by ";".
Exple : x := list new.
x add: 1.
x add: 2.
x add: 6.
x inspect.
Equivaut à écrire: x := list new add:1; add: 2; add: 6; inspect.

2-4 Blocks

A block is an object, an instance of the BlockClosure class, which is able to contain code and evaluate it contextually and on demand. Expressions in a block are not directly evaluated. It can be assigned to a variable and receive messages.
A block executes these expressions when it receives the **value** message.
Exple
:| x y |.
x := [4 + 10]. x inspect. -> a BlockClosure.
x := [4 + 10] value. x inspect. -> 14.

2-5_Control structures

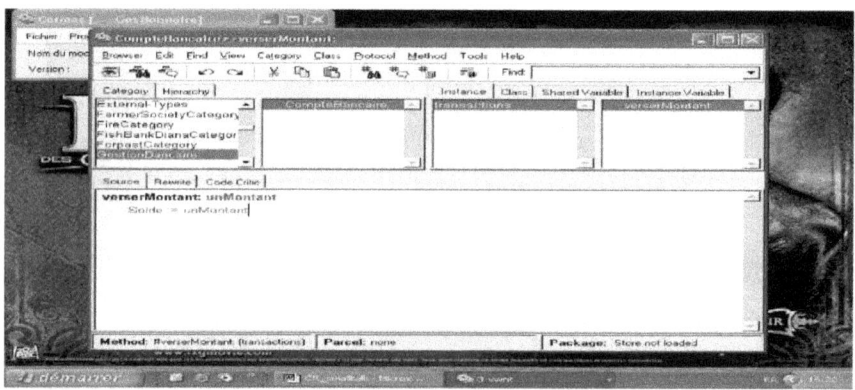

Definition of the pourAmount method.

Appendix B

Erlang

1 The development environment

To take your first steps with Erlang, you'll need to install the development environment on the official Erlang website www.erlang.org.

1-1 The virtual machine

The virtual machine is the heart of the execution environment for programs developed in Erlang. It acts as a layer of abstraction, enabling the same pseudocode binary file to be executed on different systems without recompilation. As a result, the developer has a complete, coherent environment at his disposal, freeing him from the constraints of using methods specific to an operating system.

The Erlang virtual machine known as "jam" (joe abstract machine) has been replaced by the "beam" virtual machine, which is now supplied with the development environment.

1-2 The Shell Erlang

Defined as an interface to the Erlang interpreter, the Shell is responsible for compiling, loading and executing Erlang programs. It also monitors and controls execution.

The Erlang Shell is launched with the "erl" command from the Dos. A graphical version is available for Windows. It is essentially a tool for interactive command execution. It's important to note that, from an Erlang Shell, you can use the environment's network functions to open a remote session on another Erlang virtual machine.

1-3 Source files

Erlang development requires the production of source files. These have the extension ".erl". Each source file contains code corresponding to a module (a unit of code organization grouping together several functions). Erlang application development involves defining modules which, once compiled, can be used in the interpreter.

We'll define a simple module and move on to its execution in the next section. We start by entering the following code in a text file, outside the Erlang interpreter.

```erlang
-module(bonjour).
-export([afficher/0]).
afficher() -> io:format("Bonjour tout le monde ! ",[]).
```

This code is saved in a file named "bonjour.erl". The module name must be identical to the file name.

1-4 Compilation

The "c()" function is integrated into the system and is used to compile a source file located in the current directory. It accepts the module name as a parameter. If compilation is successful, the compiler generates a pseudocode file with the module name and ".beam" extension. By default, this file is placed in the current directory.

For example, for our previous module, compilation is performed with the following command, launched from the command line with the module name "bonjour" as parameter. The interpreter must first be launched from the directory where the file is located.

```
1> c(bonjour).
   {ok,bonjour}
```
The second line indicates that compilation has been completed successfully. You can now start execution by calling the "displayQ" function, preceded by the module name.

```
2> bonjour:afficher().
   Bonjour tout le monde !
   Ok
```

2 Elementary variables and types

2-1 Integers

Integers in Erlang are not limited to a particular range of values, as is the case in low-level languages. Erlang automatically handles large numbers, without worrying about variable typing and size.
Example:

2-2 The real ones

$$X = 12345678901234567890 * 12345678901234567890.$$

This type is used to manipulate floating-point numbers, not integers. The dot is used as a decimal separator. Note also the exponential notation, which consists in representing a number with a single digit before the decimal separator. The order of magnitude is expressed by the character "E" followed by the number of times the number must be multiplied by 10 to obtain its real representation.

Example:
$Y = -4.1356$
$Z = 1234.12$ équivaut à 1.23412^E3.
$K = 0.00012$ équivaut à 1.2^E-4

2-3 Atoms

This type represents constants containing information in the form of a sequence of characters. It enables development conventions to be set up, and helps make programs more readable. Atoms are widely used for naming data structures.

An atom can contain any type of character, as long as it's enclosed in a single " ' ". Ellipses are optional if the atom begins with a lower-case letter of the alphabet and contains only alphabetic or numeric characters, or the underscore "_".

Example:
'Atome avec quottes'
atome_2_sans_quotte
atome123_trois

2-4 Process identifiers

This type shows the importance of processes and parallel development in Erlang. A process identifier is unique on an Erlang node and also across a network of interconnected Erlang virtual machines.

A process is defined by three integers, framed by the characters "<" and ">" and separated by dots ". ". Having a process identifier gives important privileges over this process. It is possible to send messages to this process, to influence its behavior or kill it.

Example: <0.23.0> ! stopped.

2-5 References

References are often used by Erlang system modules, but rarely by developers, who use them only when they need a unique identifier for all network nodes. References are generated by the built-in make_ref/0 function.

    1> X= make_ref().

Example: #ref<0.0.0.107>

2-6 Compound types and data structures

Like elementary types, compound types are very limited in number. There are two of them: lists and tuples. They can be used to model any data structure.

2-6-1 Listings

A list can contain several compound or elementary types. Square brackets "[" and "]" mark the beginning and end of a list. The elements of a list are separated by commas and are not limited.

Lists are generally used to model structures whose number of elements cannot be determined in advance. Recursion is widely used in list processing.

Example:
    N = [10, 2, 56, 67].
    T = [<0.1.0>, <0.23.0>, #ref<0.0.0.107>, true, jean].
    Listevide = [].
    ListeDeListe = [[10, 2, 56, 67], [<0.1.0>, <0.23.0>, #ref<0.0.0.107>, true, jean], [true, false, error]].

For list processing, item extraction etc., see *program listing*.

2-6-2 Tuples

Tuples, like lists, can contain several compound or elementary types. The braces "{" and "}" mark the beginning and end of a tuple. The elements of a tuple are separated by commas ",". The use of a tuple implies that you know in advance the number of elements it contains, and that you want to give meaning to each of its elements.

For more details, see *program listing*.

Example: Tuple_1 = {``Stephan``, ``Guy``, ``entraîneur``}.

2-6-3 Structures

Structures are a generalization of tuples. Basically, they enable the information conveyed in a tuple to be typed, facilitate code maintenance by avoiding major modifications, and improve code readability by enabling access to a tuple element by name. To define a data structure, we add a declaration of the form :
    -record(student,{name, surname, faculty, level}).
The first parameter defines the structure name and the second parameter defines a tuple of atoms, symbolizing the structure elements (fields).

It's important to note that whenever structure manipulation instructions are used, the compiler replaces them with instructions for equivalent tuples. The preceding record is represented by the following tuple: {student, last name, first name, faculty, level}.
The following syntax is used to access the values of a structure:
    Variable#structure_name.field_name.

The variable Variable must be linked to a structure of type structure_name, and the field is called field_name.
For illustration, see *program listing*.

2-6-3 The binary type

This type only exists in new versions of Erlang. It is primarily intended for defining network communication protocols, and enables information to be stored in binary format and binary operations to be carried out directly. This type has a number of non-negligible characteristics, notably low memory consumption compared with lists, and high processing performance. For example, passing a binary parameter to a function does not result in duplication, compared with other types.

2-7 Control structures

Unlike other languages, Erlang doesn't have many control structures, but we can develop them to suit our needs.

2-7-1 Loops

For, while and do while loops don't exist in Erlang because they don't meet a direct need, and the language has very powerful tools, such as recursion, to model every conceivable type of loop.

These are recursive functions, which are used instead of loops to avoid the edge effects so common with the latter. The following module models for and while loops:
```
-module(boucles).
-export([boucleFor/2, boucleWhile/1]).
boucleFor(Val, Val) -> ok;
boucleFor(Val1, Valn) ->
        io:format("compteur = ~p~n",[Val1]),
        boucleFor(Val1 + 1, Valn).

boucleWhile(Val)when Val =< 0 -> ok;
boucleWhile(Val) -> io:format("etape : ~p~n", [Val * 2]),
        boucleWhile(Val - 1).
```
2-7-2 Conditional processing

- the case instruction: this allows you to perform a conditional test, using pattern matching and the guards we'll see next.

Syntaxe : case Valeur of
    Motif1 -> traitement1 ;
    Motif2 -> traitement2
    end.

- The if statement: the execution condition of statement k depends on the result returned by
  Syntaxe : if Expression1 -> instruction1 ;
             Expression2 -> instruction2 ;
             Expression3 -> instruction3 ;
             true -> instruction_par_defaut
  expression k.   end.

- Guards: used to select a clause for execution. They are used, with the same syntax, for the clauses of a case statement. The guard expression can only use the following comparison operations: ==, =/=,

  Syntax :
             fonction(Val1, Val2) when Garde -> traitement ;
             Fonction(Val1, Val2) -> traitement2.

3 Erlang cookies

We illustrate this part by connecting three nodes (A, B, C) in two cases:
- All three nodes have the same *cookie magic*.
- The three nodes have different "*magic cookies*".

Case 1:
  The *cookie* is called *cookiemagic*
  Node names :
    node A-> *noeudA@mach.inei*

    node B-> *nodeB@machine2*

    node C-> *nodeC&machinez*

The three nodes reside on different machines belonging to the same network.
The large rectangle represents the Erlang node network.

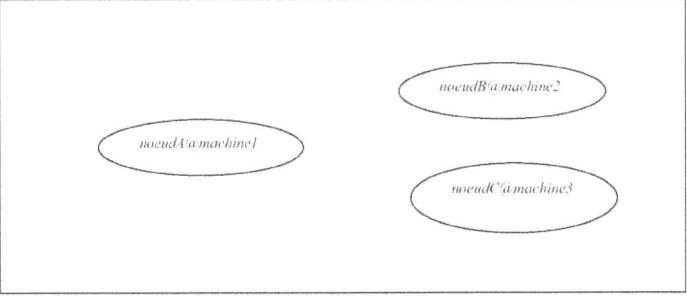

Diagram 1: network configuration

We'll now run the following commands: NodeA: *net_adm :ping('nodeB@machine2')*. Node B: *net_adm :ping('nodeC@machine3')*.

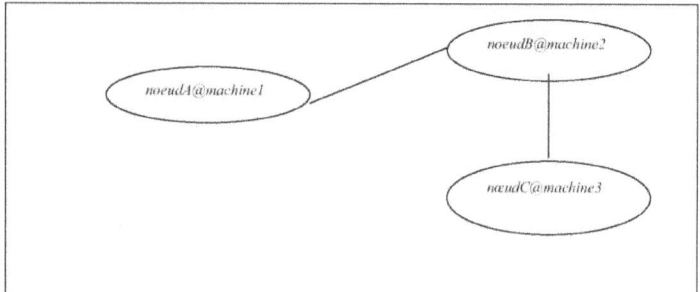

Diagram 2: connection between nodes

Diagram 2 shows the connection established explicitly, after these commands have been issued, but implicitly, the result of the connection is shown in diagram 3.

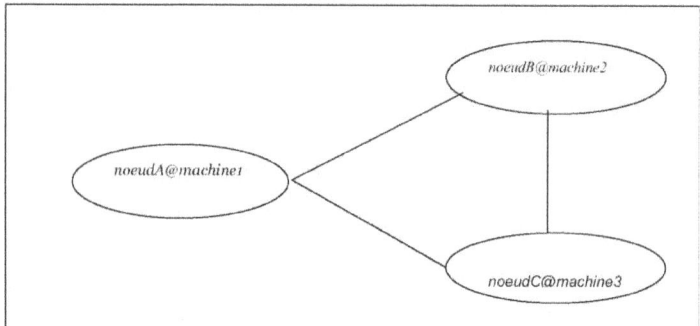

Diagram 3: identical cookies

Results :
We notice a transitivity, which is established if the nodes have the same "*cookie magic*". If node A is friends with node B and B is friends with C, then A and C are friends.

- case 2 :
Now the nodes have different *cookies*.
Node names :
    node A-> *noeudA@mach.inei* cookie -> *cookA*

    node B-> *nodeB@machine2* cookie -> *cookB*
    node C-> *nodeC&machine^* cookie -> *cookC*
In this new scenario, it is essential to negotiate friendship between the different nodes in order to initiate communication between them.

For node A to communicate with node B, it must know node B's *cookie*.
The following command is run on node A:
  erlang :set_cookie('nodeB@machine2', 'cookB').
As this concept of friendship is reflexive, the *net_kernel* system process sends node B the *cookie* from node A, and the friendship between these two nodes is established.
We do the same between node B and node C :
  Erlang :set_cookie('nodeC@machine3', 'cookC').
The friendship between node B and node C is thus established.
The configuration shown in Figure 4 is obtained if the following commands are run:
  NodeA: *net_adm :ping('nodeB@machine2')*.
  Node B: *net_adm :ping('nodeC@machine3')*.

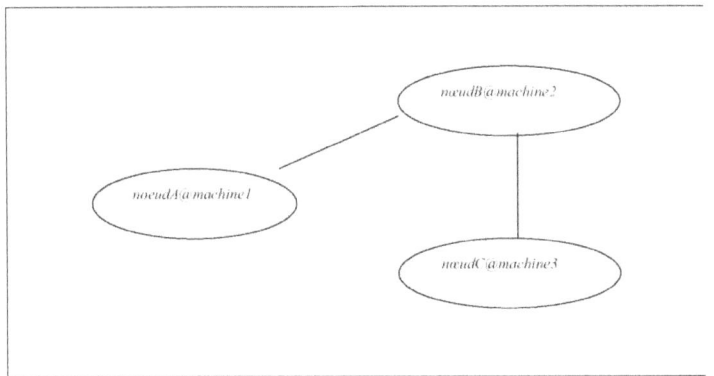

Figure 4: different cookies

Interestingly, the transitivity that existed in the first case is no longer respected. The friendship between node A and node C must therefore be explicitly established.

References

[Amstrong et al. 1996] J. Amstrong, R. Virding, C. Wikstrom and M. Williams "concurrent programming in Erlang", Ericsson Telecom System Laboratories, Sweden. www.erlang.se

[Arthursson et al. 1997] J. Arthursson, J. Engblom, M. Jonsson, R. Mirza, M. Schimid, B. Spolader, E. Zolfonoom, "A Platform for Secure Mobiles Agents", Medialab/ Computer Science Lab Ericsson Telecom, Stockholm,Sweden.

[Barreiro et al. 2001] M. Barreiro, J.L. Freire, V.M. Gulias and J.J. Sanchez, "Exploiting Sequential Libraries on a Cluster of Computers", LFCIA, Dept of Computer Science University of A Coruna, Spain.

[Dacker, 2000] B. Dacker "concurrent functional programming for telecommunications: case study of technology introduction", computer system laboratory, royal institute of technology Stockholm, Sweden.

[Carlsson et al. 2003] R. Carlsson, K. Sagonas and J. Wilkhelmssom, "Message Analysis of Concurrent Language", Computing Science Dept, Uppsala University, Sweden.

[Carlsson and Millroth, 1999] R. Carlsson and H. Millroth, "On Cyclic Processes dependencies and the Verification of Absence of Deadlocks in Reactive System", Computing Science Dept, Uppsala University, Sweden. www.csd.uu.se

[Castro, 2001] M. Castro, "Erlang in Real Time", Dept of Computer Science, RMIT Melbourne, Australia. www.rmit.edu.au

[Ferber 1995p. Ferber "Les systèmes multi-agents - vers une intelligence collective", Intereditions, Paris.

[Giesl and Arts, 2001] J. Giesl and T. Arts, "Verification of Erlang Processes by Dependency Pairs", Computer Science Dept University of new Mexico USA, Computer Science Lab Ericsson Utvecklings AB, Sweden. www.artes.uu.se

[Ginot et al. 2002] V. Ginot, G. Le Page, S. Souissi, "A multi-agent architecture to enhance end-user individual-based modelling", INRA-Unite de Biometrie domaine St Paul Avignon, CIRAD-Land and Resources Programme Montpellier, Ecosystem Complexity Research Group-Université des Sciences et Technologies de Lille, CNRS- UPRES Wimereux, France.

[Grafstrom and Aronsson, 1995] J. Grafstrom and T. Aronsson, "A Comparaison beetwen Erlang an C++ for Implementation of Telecom Applications", Ericsson Telecom AB, Sweden.

[Hedqvist, 1998] P. Hedqvist, "A parallel and Multithreaded erlang Implementation", Computing Science Dept, Uppsala University, Sweden.

[Johansson, 2003] E. Johansson, "Hipe Technical Reference", Computing Science Dept, Uppsala University, Sweden.

[Johansson et al. 2002] E. Johansson, M. Pettersson, K. Sagonas, T. Lindgren, "The Development ofThe Hipe System: Design and Experience Report", Computing Science Dept (Uppsala University, Sweden), Bluetail AB (Stockholm, Sweden).

[Johansson, 1999] E. Johansson, "Performance Measurements and processes Optimization for Erlang", Computer Science Dept, Uppsala University, Sweden.

[Johansson et al 99] E. Johansson, S. Nystrom, T. Lindgren and C. Jonsson, "Evaluation of Hipe an Erlang Native Code Compiler", Computing Science Dept (Uppsala University, Sweden), Bluetail AB (Stockholm, Sweden), Apicula(Stockholm, Sweden). [Johansson et al. 1999] E. Johansson, S. Nystrom, M. Pettersson, and K. Sagonas, "HIPE: High Performance Erlang", Computing Science Dept, Uppsala University, Sweden.

[Karlsson, 2000] B. Karlsson, "Secure Distributed Communication in SafeErlang" Dept ofTeleinformatics, The Royal Institute ofTechnology. www.kth.se

[Lindgren et al. 1997] A. Lindgren, A. Bottena and T. Lindgren, "A High Precision Measurement Tool for Erlang", Computing Science Dept, Uppsala University, Sweden.

[Mattsson et al. 1998] H. Mattsson, H Nilsson and C. Wikstrom. Wikstrom, "Mnesia a Distributed robust DBMS for Telecm Application", Computer Science Lab Ericsson Telecom AB, Stockholm,Sweden.

[Nystrom and Johnson, 2002] J. Nystrom and B. Johnson, "extracting the processes structure of Erlang application". Johnson, "extracting the processes structure of Erlang application", Dept of Computer Systems, Dept of Information Technology, Uppsala University, Sweden. www.csd.uu.se

[Paul et al. 2002] B. Paul, B. Pascal, B. Mathieu and F. Eric, "Les systemes multiagents", EPITA, 2002.

[Remond, 2003] M. Remond, "Erlang programmation" Eyrolles, 2003. www.erlang-fr.org and www.erlang.org

[Villeneuve, 2003] B.Villeneuve, "Modélisation individus-centree de stratégies adaptatives des populations de poissons en réponse aux pressions de l'environnement en milieu estuarien", UR-RAP, IRD Sénégal.

I want morebooks!

Buy your books fast and straightforward online - at one of world's fastest growing online book stores! Environmentally sound due to Print-on-Demand technologies.

Buy your books online at
www.morebooks.shop

Kaufen Sie Ihre Bücher schnell und unkompliziert online – auf einer der am schnellsten wachsenden Buchhandelsplattformen weltweit! Dank Print-On-Demand umwelt- und ressourcenschonend produziert.

Bücher schneller online kaufen
www.morebooks.shop

 info@omniscriptum.com
www.omniscriptum.com

Ingram Content Group UK Ltd.
Milton Keynes UK
UKHW040733260623
424053UK00001B/179